COLIN POWELL

Other Books in the **Today's Heroes** Series

Ben Carson

As a kid his knife was a weapon—now he uses it to save lives.

Billy Graham

He grew up just a normal kid. How did he become the world's best known preacher?

Dave Dravecky

He made it in the big leagues, but then the doctor gave him bad news.

Joni's Story

When Joni Eareckson learned she'd never walk again, she wanted to die. Little did she know what was in store.

by David Roth

abridged and edited by Linda Lee Maifair and Lori Walburg

ZondervanPublishingHouse

Grand Rapids, Michigan

A Division of HarperCollinsPublishers

Colin Powell
Abridged from the book *Sacred Honor*
Sacred Honor copyright © 1993 by David Roth
Abridgment copyright © 1993 by Zondervan Publishing House

Requests for information should be addressed to:
Zondervan Publishing House
Grand Rapids, Michigan 49530

Library of Congress Cataloging-in-Publication Data

Roth, David, 1955–
    Colin Powell / David Roth and Linda Lee Maifair.
        p.   cm.   —(Today's heroes)
    ISBN 0-310-39851-7
    1. Powell, Colin L.—Juvenile literature. 2. Generals—United States—
Biography—Juvenile literature. 3. Afro-American generals—Biography—
Juvenile literature. 4. United States. Army—Biography—Juvenile literature.
[1. Powell, Colin L. 2. Generals. 3. Afro-Americans—Biography.] I. Maifair,
Linda Lee. II. Title. III. Series: Today's heroes series.
E840.5.P68R66   1993
355'.0092—dc20   93-27029
[B]   CIP
                                                                                          AC

Abridged by Linda Lee Maifair
Edited by Lori J. Walburg
Interior designed by Rachel Hostetter
Cover and interior illustrations by Patrick Kelley
Cover design by Mark Veldheer

Printed in the United States of America

93 94 95 96 97 / LP / 10 9 8 7 6 5 4 3 2

CONTENTS

Chronology of Events

April 5, 1937. Colin Luther Powell is born in Harlem, New York City.

1954. Powell graduates from Morris High School, Bronx, New York, and enters City College of New York.

1955. Powell joins the Reserve Officers Training Corps (ROTC).

1958. Powell graduates from CCNY with a degree in geology. A second lieutenant in the army, he goes to Georgia for basic training and is sent on his first tour of duty to West Germany.

1962. Powell marries Alma Johnson.

1963. Captain Powell earns a Purple Heart in Vietnam.

1968. Major Powell sent on second tour of duty in Vietnam.

1971. Powell earns a master's degree in business administration at George Washington University in Washington, D.C.

1972. Powell is named a White House Fellow.

1973. Lieutenant Colonel Powell sent on tour of duty in Korea.

1975. Powell attends the National War College in Washington, D.C.

1976–82. Holding various posts, Powell achieves rank of major general.

1983–86. Powell serves as military aide to secretary of defense and becomes a lieutenant general.

1987–89. Powell serves as national security adviser to President Reagan.

October 1, 1989. General Powell is named chairman of the Joint Chiefs of Staff.

1990–91. General Powell oversees successful operation of Desert Shield and Desert Storm.

1993. General Powell retires from the army.

Colin Powell

1

Weekend at Camp David

General Colin Powell looked on as William Jefferson Clinton was sworn in to be America's forty-second president. January 20, 1993 was a bitterly cold morning in Washington. The crowd watched, shivering, as one generation of leaders left the White House to be replaced by a younger one. Between the two administrations and two generations stood Colin Powell.

Dignitaries sat in the reviewing stand waiting for the arrival of the new First Family. Among them, Colin Powell, the chairman of the Joint Chiefs of Staff, sat with his wife beside him, looking ahead with a solemn gaze.

Two months earlier, on Tuesday, November 3, 1992, Bill Clinton defeated George Bush, signaling an end to twelve years of Republican presidency. Two days later the phone rang in Quarters 6, and Colin Powell answered it. It was Barbara Bush calling. "Hi, Colin, how are you?" she asked. The general called to Alma to get on the phone. They chatted, and Barbara asked them to join the Bushes for the weekend at Camp David. The president could be heard in the background yelling, "Tell them to bring the kids."

Jane was asleep when Mike Powell came home late and slipped into bed. "Your mom called, and she wants us to go to Camp David with the Bushes tomorrow," Jane groggily mumbled.

"What?" Mike said, astonished. The next day Alma called the White House just to be certain the invitation stood.

Alma and the family drove the two hours from Washington to Camp David, while General Powell, who had been out of town, flew in by helicopter. The Powells arrived and parked, their timing perfect. Colin's helicopter had just landed. The Powell family climbed into golf carts for the ride to the compound. They hadn't gone far when they turned a corner and there stood Barbara Bush. She wore a comfortable winter parka, and her two dogs were beside her. They chatted briefly, and Mrs. Bush invited everyone to the president's private cabin.

They sat around the fire talking, while Colin Powell's first grandchild, Jeffrey, played with blocks at their feet. The phone rang, and Mrs. Bush picked it up. It was the president. "The Powells are here," she said. "Get on up here."

A few minutes later Bush arrived. The smiling host greeted everyone. "Who's up for a walk?" he asked.

The Powells stopped at the three lavishly decorated cabins where they would spend the night. Bicycles were parked out front for each guest. Nobody was left out. In front of the cabin assigned to Mike, Jane, and Jeffrey Powell were a big man's bike with a crossbar, a medium-size woman's bike with a low bar, and a tiny two-wheel bike with training wheels just right for a four-year-old.

After dropping their bags, everyone donned parkas and set out for the woods. Snow covered the ground, but the trails were clear. The president and Chairman Powell walked out front, with George Bush setting a brisk pace. Barbara, Alma, Mike, Jane, Anne, Jeffrey, and the dogs followed behind. For an hour and a half, they walked and chatted comfortably. After another stop by the cabins to freshen up, everyone gathered in the main lodge where the president has his office and where official meetings are held.

The Bushes and the Powells gathered cozily around a single round table in the dining room.

Dinner was Texas steak. The president was called away from the table several times, as the phone rang constantly.

Bush seemed to have enormous energy. He talked about the election without any bitterness. The world had changed, he noted. He and Barbara felt that they had grown too old-fashioned for America.

The Powells asked about Bush's children and grandchildren. Bush mentioned possibly seeing a movie and complained about how movies had become so violent in recent years. Finished with his meal, Bush jumped up from his seat to move on to the next activity.

Jeffrey, still working on his ice cream, exclaimed, "I'm not done yet!"

The president of the United States sat back down. "Oh, Jeffrey's not done," he said. And Jeffrey finished his ice cream.

After dinner the Powells and the Bushes watched a movie. The next morning everyone gathered once again for breakfast. The president's brother and family from New York dropped by. As the day unfolded, Barbara was on the phone, trying to line up meetings with real estate agents in Houston. President Bush loaded Jeffrey down with presidential yo-yos, flashlights, and pens and showed him some of his own collection of keepsakes—ships and planes. The Powells decided to beat the snow that was forecast and drove south for Virginia just before sundown.

Colin Powell and George Bush had become friends over many years of working together. Bush had confidence in Powell because of his character, integrity, patriotism, and reliable performance of duty.

Three other presidents have respected and trusted Colin Powell for the same reasons. When Colin Powell talks to the most powerful people in the world, they listen. When he addresses the American people, as he did during the Gulf War and Desert Storm, they believe him. Colin Powell's character and integrity took him from the streets of the Bronx to the halls of the White House and made him a modern hero.

2

The Boys
on Kelly Street

Growing up in the South Bronx in the late forties and early fifties, Colin Powell had no TV, no VCR, no video games. But he and the other boys on Kelly Street had no trouble keeping busy.

If there wasn't too much traffic, Colin and his friends played stickball in the streets, using manhole covers for home plate and second base. They'd get together on an empty lot for a game of baseball or football. They played punchball, stoopball, hide-and-seek, and a game called "hot beans and butter." They'd divide into teams and play ring-a-levio, trying to capture the other side's men and free their own.

Colin and his friends didn't have money for a lot of fancy toys, so they made their own. They made "shooting checkers" from bottle caps filled with wax and played "Sluggo" with marbles and cigar boxes. They flew homemade razor-tail kites from the roofs of their apartment houses. And on Saturday mornings, a quarter would get them into the Tiffany Theatre, where they could spend the whole day watching cowboy movies.

One of Colin's favorite pastimes was "making the walk" around the neighborhood. "The walk" would start and end at the corner of Kelly and 163rd streets, taking the boys past a Jewish bakery, a Puerto Rican grocery store, and a Chinese laundry. There was a candy store on almost every block and a toy store on almost every corner.

Along the way, the boys would stop to peer into the big storefront windows. They'd brag about what they'd buy if they only had the money. They'd point at the huge salamis hanging from ceiling hooks in the local butcher shop. They'd take deep breaths, drawing in the pungent aromas of the wheels and wedges of cheese at the corner deli. They'd try to guess the numbers of apples or string beans in the big bins and baskets of fresh fruits and vegetables at the produce vendor's stand.

Colin Powell was one of the younger kids on Kelly Street—a couple of years behind most of the others. To a boy who had no brothers of his own, it

The Boys on Kelly Street   15

was almost like having a bunch of big brothers who let him tag along wherever they went. The older boys watched out for Colin, and they didn't let him get into trouble—even when they did.

Colin liked to collect stamps, read, and make maps. But he'd rather be outside playing ball with his friends than sitting inside doing homework. He was an average student. In fourth grade, he was placed in the slow class, and the report cards he carried home weren't nearly as good as his older sister's.

Colin came from a strict but loving family who believed in honesty, faith, hard work, and education. Colin's father, Luther Powell, had immigrated to America from Jamaica, a British colony in the West Indies. His family had been peasant farmers. He left behind his parents and seven brothers and sisters when he moved to New York City and settled in Harlem.

Small, brown-faced Luther Powell was a generous man with a strong faith. In Jamaica, his family had belonged to the Anglican Church—the Church of England. Now, settled in New York City, he found a church home in St. Phillip's Episcopal Church, the American branch of the Church of England. He loved the high church liturgy and the clear peals of church bells because they reminded him of his family in Jamaica. But it was his quiet faith in God and his hard work and discipline that carried him through difficult days as an immigrant during the Depression.

In the summer of 1927, Luther went to church picnics held at Pelham Bay Park. Finally, at one of the picnics, he worked up the nerve to approach a young, pretty Jamaican immigrant named Maud. They were married almost two years later.

Maud had graduated from high school, but Luther hadn't. Sometimes, when Maud got annoyed with Luther, she'd mutter an insult: "Him who never finished high school."

But both Maud and Luther valued hard work and education. They always had newspapers and books lying about, and they often told Colin and his older sister, Marilyn, "Strive for a good education. Make something of your life."

Even though Luther didn't have the opportunity to go to school, he proved himself as a hard worker. He left for work early each morning and didn't return until seven or eight at night. In his job in the garment industry, he worked his way up, one step at a time. From a warehouseman to a shipping clerk. From a shipping clerk to head of the shipping department. From shipping department to foreman.

Maud worked also, as a seamstress for a Manhattan garment company. A "finisher," she would sew on buttons and trim. Every Thursday night she counted up her week's tickets—each one snipped from the garments she had worked on—and bundled them with rubber bands. The next morning she took them downtown to get her pay.

Like his parents, Colin Powell began working early. One day, when he was about thirteen, he happened to be walking by Sickser's—a store specializing in baby cribs, strollers, carriages, and toys—when the owner, Mr. Sickser, stepped out the front door and looked up and down the sidewalk.

When he saw Colin, Mr. Sickser motioned to the boy. "I need some extra help unloading some boxes," he said. "How would you like to make a little money?"

"Yes, sir," Colin said, his eyes lighting up. He didn't get many chances to make money. He followed Mr. Sickser into the store. The next few hours, he unloaded boxes and cheerfully did whatever odd jobs Mr. Sickser asked him to do.

Mr. Sickser was impressed by Colin's hard work and positive attitude. "You're a good worker," he told him at the end of the day. "If you want to come back next weekend, I might be able to find more work for you to do."

Colin came back to Sickser's the next weekend, and just about every weekend for the next five years. During the school year he would put in twelve to fifteen hours a week at the store, earning fifty to seventy-five cents an hour. Most of the work was general labor, doing whatever needed to be done at the time.

Colin helped to put together the cribs and strollers. He unloaded trucks. He unpacked boxes and boxed merchandise for shipment. He helped to make deliveries. And he set up special sale displays at Christmastime. He was a good worker. He always showed up on time. He was polite to his customers and coworkers. And he worked very hard. He kept his job at Sickser's until he was a sophomore in college.

Colin grew up in a neighborhood where his neighbors and friends came from many different races and backgrounds. On Kelly Street, everybody was a minority—blacks, Puerto Ricans, Jews, Irish, and Italians. No one received special treatment, and all the different races got along. At Sickser's, Colin even learned a little Yiddish from his Jewish coworkers! But in high school, Colin took a job at a Coca-Cola bottling plant. There, things were different.

Colin soon learned that whites were in the majority, and they received better jobs. The white kids worked on the bottling machine, making more money than the black kids, who mopped floors.

Colin made ninety cents an hour mopping floors. But he didn't resent the work, and he didn't complain. He just did the job the best that he could. Years later he still talks about how hard he worked

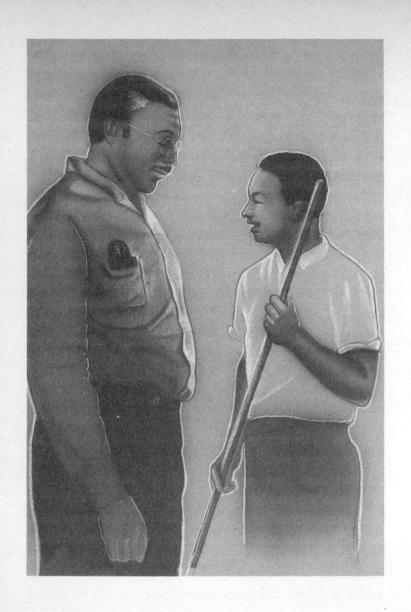

at that bottling plant job. "When somebody comes and dumps about fifty cases of cola on the floor, I want to tell you, that is some serious mopping!" he says. With a lot of slippery, sticky soda on the floor, Colin quickly learned there was a right way and a wrong way to mop floors. Not just sloshing the mop around but working back and forth, back and forth. Left to right. Right to left. He got a lot of practice that summer, and he learned to mop well.

His work didn't go unnoticed. At the end of the summer, the plant foreman went up to Colin and said, "You mop floors pretty good."

"You sure gave me enough opportunity to learn, sir," Colin told him.

"Why don't you come back next summer?" the foreman suggested.

"To do what?" Colin asked. He'd had enough of mopping floors. He thought he deserved the right to try something better.

Like Mr. Sickser, the foreman was impressed with Colin's work. "We're going to put you on the machine," he promised.

The next summer Colin went back to the bottling plant. This time, he didn't have to mop floors. He worked on the filling machine. And he made more money. At first he just took the bottles out and put them on the conveyor belt. By the end of the summer, he was one of the top kids on the machine's inspection crew. The next summer, Colin went back again. This time he had worked his way up to a deputy machine foreman.

Every time he was given a job, Colin thought of it as an opportunity to show what he could do. No matter what sort of job it was, he did whatever he was asked to do. And he did it the best that he could. He worked hard, and he didn't complain.

His attitude toward work never failed to impress his employers. And that attitude earned him promotion after promotion. Finally, Colin Powell, the "average" kid from Kelly Street, became the chairman of the Joint Chiefs of Staff, the highest ranking soldier in all of America's armed services.

3

Making Choices

By the time Colin Powell became a teenager, the neighborhood around Kelly Street had changed. Most of the changes were not good ones. Stores were closing. People were moving out. The teenagers in South Bronx were divided into two groups—those who took drugs and those who didn't.

On every street corner, drug dealers pushed marijuana and heroin. "Give it a try," they'd say to the teenagers. "There's nothing like it. It'll make you feel good."

Some of Colin's friends fell for the sales pitch. Some even tried to get him to take drugs. "Just take a puff," they'd say, holding out a joint.

Colin shook his head. "My parents would kill me," he said. He loved his parents and didn't want to do anything to disappoint them.

"Aw, who cares what your parents think? Try it!" his friends persisted. "Just see how it makes you feel!"

"I don't care how it makes me feel," Colin said. "Drugs are stupid." And he turned and walked away. He didn't care if "everyone" was using drugs, because his best friends, Gene Norman and Tony Grant, weren't.

Today General Powell tells teenagers, "Using drugs is the most self-destructive thing you can do with the life that God and your parents have given you. Of all the kids I grew up with on Kelly Street, Gene Norman and one or two others made it. Too many of the others did not make it. They went to jail, or they died, or they were never heard from again."

Colin hung around with other teens who weren't into drugs. He kept himself busy with school. He got involved in church activities. He used his spare time to earn money with part-time jobs. And he and Gene Norman spent a lot of time exploring New York City together.

They looked forward to getting their two-wheeled bicycles the way teenagers today look forward to getting their own cars. The bikes gave them a freedom they hadn't known before. On their bikes, they could travel far beyond their Kelly Street neighborhood. Gene and Colin would ride as far out as Pelham Bay Park and back again or race each other down Hunt Point's steep Bank Note Hill.

For a nickel, they could take a trolley almost anywhere in the city. Sometimes they'd take the trolley to the George Washington Bridge. Then they'd walk across the bridge from New York to New Jersey, where they'd camp out together overnight in the woods.

Colin liked camping and other outdoor activities. For a while, he made the long trip to New Jersey to belong to a Scout troop there. But Colin did not stay in Boy Scouts long. Unfortunately, as the only black youth in the troop, Colin did not feel welcome. He decided that the long trip to New Jersey and back wasn't worth it.

Because the Powells wanted their children to attend college, both Marilyn and Colin took the college-preparatory courses at Morris High. The other kids liked Colin, but he was never one of the most popular students. Colin says he "horsed around" a lot in high school, but he stayed out of trouble. He ran cross-country on the track team and enjoyed his work with the Service League.

Colin graduated from high school after three and a half years. Even though he had only a C average, he was accepted by both the City College of New York and New York University. He had no trouble choosing which college to attend. Tuition at NYU was $750 a year. Tuition at CCNY was $10. Colin enrolled at CCNY in February 1954, two months before his seventeenth birthday.

A freshman in college at only sixteen, Colin wasn't sure what he wanted to study. He didn't even know what he wanted to do with his life. Today he tells teens to stay in school, stay away from drugs, work hard, have a goal or vision for your life, and stick to it. But it took the young Colin Powell a little while to set his own goals and find his own vision.

He went to college mainly because his parents expected it. He wasn't sure what he should do, or what he wanted to be. His mother gave him some practical advice. "Take engineering," she told him when it was time to register for classes. "That's where the money is."

Colin chose engineering as his major. On a cold, wintry day in February, he skipped breakfast and took a bus across the 155th Street bridge. He rode up the hill, anxious, excited—and hungry. When he got off the bus, he spotted Raymond the Bagelman, a well-known character on campus. Quickly he bought a fresh, warm bagel before mounting the steps of CCNY.

Colin worked hard and averaged a B in his first semester, but a mechanical drawing class that summer was a disaster. One hot day in June, when the instructor asked him to describe a cone

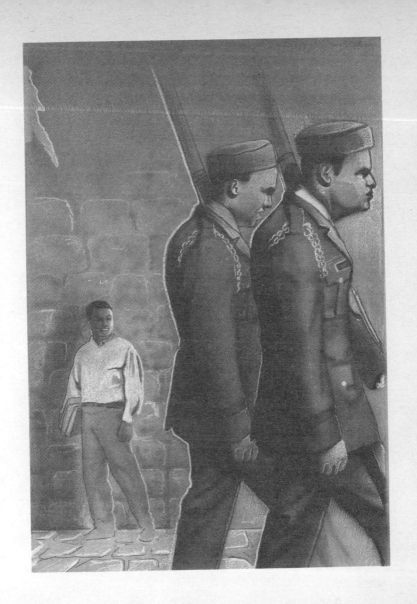

intersecting a plane in space, Colin's mind went blank. Flustered and sweating, he finally said, "I don't know how."

That summer was the worst of Colin's life. He decided to drop his engineering major, and he had serious doubts about staying in college. But he didn't want to disappoint his parents. So he switched his major to geology.

As the school year wore on, Colin struggled through physics, calculus, geology, and history. He didn't excel at anything. But one day Colin noticed a bunch of students walking down Amsterdam and Convent avenues in uniforms. They were members of the local ROTC (Reserve Officer Training Corps) detachment at CCNY. Colin was impressed by them. He liked the way they looked—especially the elite group, called Pershing Rifles, who wore small whipped cords on their uniform shoulders.

Colin joined the ROTC at City College. Finally, he had found his niche. For the first time ever, he made A's in his course work for the ROTC. And he thought it was fun! He had found his goal: to become an officer in the U.S. Army.

His mother, who had wanted him to be an engineer, or a minister, or even a geologist, wasn't so sure. She didn't really like the idea of her only son going into the army, but she didn't stand in his way.

Years later, Colin Powell's youngest daughter,

Linda, told her father she wanted to go to acting school. It wasn't what he had in mind for her, either. And he knew acting wasn't the easiest or most practical career to follow. But he knew she too needed to have the chance to find her own special niche in life. He agreed to send her to acting school. He hoped that finding the right goal—finding something that she liked and really wanted to succeed at—might turn out as well for her as it had for him when he joined ROTC.

4

Learning to Be a Soldier

Colin Powell never felt very comfortable in his regular college courses. His overall average was barely more than a C. He didn't feel he had much talent for academic subjects. He didn't find them very interesting or practical.

ROTC was different. He enjoyed it, did well, and never felt like he was wasting his time. He earned a straight-A average in his military subjects, and some of the men he met in ROTC remain lifelong friends. Joining the ROTC marked a turning point in Colin's life.

Some of Colin's college classmates at CCNY

thought ROTC was "square," dull, and out of date. They couldn't see why anyone would want to spend his time doing drills and marches. But Colin liked the order and the discipline. That's what he'd grown up with at home—rules and responsibilities.

In ROTC classes, Colin Powell learned drill and ceremonies. He studied army procedures, map reading, and basic infantry tactics. He practiced rifle marksmanship. In the summers he went to a camp where the skills he'd learned in the classroom were put to practical use.

As soon as he could, Colin joined the Pershing Rifles—the best and most serious of the ROTC students. While some of the students had joined the ROTC program to avoid being drafted, Pershing Rifle cadets were more likely to be thinking of making the army a full-time career. Powell and his Pershing Rifles friends were the clean-cut, "good kids" on campus. They enjoyed a good party now and then, but they stayed out of serious trouble.

Every young person needs someone to look up to—a role model to follow. Today General Powell is that kind of role model for thousands of American children and teenagers. But in the ROTC, Colin's role model was a young man named Ronnie Brooks.

Ronnie Brooks was a Pershing Rifles member two years older than Colin Powell. Colin looked up to him and followed his example. He also followed

Brooks into every position he held in the Pershing Rifles, including the top spot of company commander. Ronnie taught Colin how to lead by example. Instead of telling people what to do or how to act, Ronnie showed them by doing it himself. Many years later, Colin put Ronnie's lesson to good use in Korea, Vietnam, and the deserts of Saudi Arabia.

As a junior just beginning the ROTC advanced program, Colin was put in charge of recruiting new members for the Pershing Rifles. One of the twenty-one new members he initiated was freshman Tony Mavroudis. Like Colin Powell had done with Ronnie Brooks, Tony Mavroudis followed Colin Powell's example. When Colin's family moved from the South Bronx into Queens, Tony lived nearby. They became close friends.

The two young men hung around together. They double dated and learned about girls. Colin stayed at Tony's house and called his parents Mom and Dad, and Tony did the same with Colin's parents. They were good kids, but they weren't perfect. In the two years before Colin graduated, they managed to destroy both of their fathers' cars.

When Colin Powell graduated from CCNY in June 1958, he was Pershing Rifles company commander with the rank of cadet colonel. He was also designated a Distinguished Military graduate. He was now an officer in the army.

A few days later, the new second lieutenant left New York City. He climbed aboard a Greyhound bus and headed south for Fort Benning, Georgia, where he would begin his military career.

His mother still couldn't quite accept the idea of her only son becoming a full-time soldier. Waving good-bye, she called, "Do your two years. Come home. You'll get a job. You'll be all right."

But Colin Powell already had a job . . . a job he would do very well for the next thirty-five years.

At Fort Benning, home of the United States Army Infantry, Colin learned to be a soldier. For five months, he and the other new lieutenants studied small unit tactics. Some things, like establishing a perimeter defense or the offensive use of a rifle, were exciting. Some things, like learning how to fill out government forms and ordering supplies, were not. But all of it was important.

Lieutenant Powell tinkered with jeeps and manned the radios. He practiced handling "prisoners of war" and found out how to escape if he were taken prisoner himself. Out in the wilds of Georgia, he learned to navigate by night or day, with or without a compass. He learned survival skills and practiced shooting small arms, especially the rifle. In mock battles, he fought other soldiers in close, hand-to-hand combat situations. Sweating from the sticky Georgia heat, he pushed himself through physically demanding obstacle courses and outdoor field training exercises. Many young officers-in-training dropped left and right from the heat—"heat casualties," they were called. But no matter how hot it got, Lieutenant Powell always managed to squeeze out a smile, tell a joke, and drive on.

When he finished his basic training, Lieutenant Powell was ordered to attend both the Ranger and Airborne training schools. An order to go to either special training is considered an honor. Both are difficult and demanding.

The three-week Airborne course involved lots of punishing, humiliating, and repetitive physical training. Trainees ran from place to place all day long, only stopping long enough to drop down and do push-ups or sit-ups. Every day before sunrise, they stood in long rows for inspection, their shoes freshly spit-shined.

To learn to parachute, they practiced landing falls. They jumped from mock airplane doors. They practiced counting—"one thousand, two thousand, three thousand, four thousand"—and learned to check for an open canopy. Then they jumped from a thirty-foot high practice tower and a 250-foot high gondola. Finally, in the end, they parachuted from real aircraft. Colin learned how to jump out of an airplane, land safely, and go on with the work of an infantry officer on the ground. When he finished the course, he had "earned his wings."

From Airborne training, Lieutenant Powell went

Colin Powell

on to Ranger training. Ranger school is an extended, magnified version of all that is muddiest, sweatiest, most tiring, and taxing in the infantryman's life in the field. Powell spent long-range night patrols wading through muddy streams and slogging through chilly swamps filled with snakes and snapping turtles. He marched for hours under the baking sun, carrying a sixty-pound field pack, with a rifle slung over his shoulder and a steel pot on his head. For weeks, Powell lived on very little food and snatches of sleep.

On one all-night patrol, Powell's unit set out into the darkness of the swamp. Their assignment: keep moving all night. As the tallest men in the unit, Powell and a friend, Bill McCaffrey, carried the heavy, bulky machine guns instead of the regular M-1 rifles. But the soldiers in Powell's unit had been taught teamwork. They were supposed to look out for each other—and that included helping each other carry the heaviest guns. Soldiers carrying rifles were expected to take turns carrying the machine guns.

The long night hours crawled by. The guns grew heavier and heavier. Finally, at 3:00 A.M., another soldier tapped Powell on the shoulder. He would take the machine gun.

Relieved and grateful, Colin pulled the gun from his shoulder. Immediately he felt lighter—free.

He took the man's rifle. The difference in weight was amazing. He felt like he could march all night.

But then he turned and saw his friend, Bill, still burdened with his machine gun. No one had offered to trade his rifle for Bill's heavy weapon. Without saying a word, Colin handed Bill the rifle and took on his machine gun. Then he turned and marched off into the night.

Many soldiers fail to complete Airborne training. Many fail to finish Ranger school. Colin Powell finished both courses. Then, in October 1958, he set off for Germany, his first "real army" assignment.

Lieutenant Powell was assigned to guard a section of the Fulda Gap. At that time Germany was still divided into East and West by the Berlin Wall. The United States and Russia were rivals and enemies in what was known as the cold war. If the Soviets decided to move into central Europe, they would come through the Fulda Gap. Through the bitter cold and biting winds of the winters of 1958–59 and 1959–60, Powell and his men sat in M59 armored personnel carriers, waiting and watching and looking eastward. Across the Gap, the men of the Soviet Eighth Guards Army sat waiting and watching and looking back at them.

In Germany, as always, Powell worked his way up from one assignment to the next. He did whatever job he was given as well as he could. He

Colin Powell

led a rifle platoon. He was put in charge of the company's heavy mortars. He even served as a company executive officer, working for the company commander. In each case, his service was exemplary. Two days before New Year's Day of 1960, he was promoted to first lieutenant.

5

A Different Kind of Fight

Just before Thanksgiving, 1961, Alma Johnson's roommate told her, "I met this really nice guy. He's coming in this weekend and he's bringing a friend."

The "really nice guy" was a lieutenant from nearby Fort Devens. The "friend" was Colin Powell, who had been reassigned back in the United States.

"I don't go on blind dates," Alma told Jacqueline. She turned and walked from the room.

As the weekend got closer, Jacqueline kept pestering her about the date. "Look," Alma said, facing her roommate with her hands on her hips. "I don't go on blind dates. And I definitely do not go out with soldiers. How do I know what might be walking through the door?"

"He'll be nice, you'll see," Jacqueline argued.

"Forget it," Alma said. "I'm going out that night anyway."

"No, you're not," Jacqueline said. "You're staying right here. And you're going on a double date with me."

They argued for a long time, and finally Alma gave in. But secretly she decided that this soldier—whoever he was—would be sorry he came to meet her. Hoping to turn him off, she dressed in a tight dress and put on a lot of heavy makeup. When the knock came at the door and she heard her roommate talking with the two soldiers, she made her grand entrance.

Lieutenant Powell and Alma looked at each other—both surprised. Powell had rosy cheeks from the cold, a very close haircut, and looked about twelve years old. "Who is this baby?" Alma thought to herself.

They sat and chatted a while. In spite of the way Alma was dressed, Powell treated her respectfully. After a while, Alma decided that "this baby" was really a very nice young man.

"Excuse me for a minute," she said, blushing slightly. "I'll be right back."

While her friends waited, Alma changed into a

more conservative dress and washed the makeup off her face. Then the two couples went to a nightclub and out for a bite to eat. At the end of the evening, Alma agreed to see the young lieutenant again the next weekend. Before long, their weekend visits back and forth became a steady thing.

Not long after they met, Alma asked Colin, "How long do you plan to stay in the army?" Most of the young men she knew in the army had been drafted and couldn't wait to get out.

"I'm making it a career," Colin told her.

Alma shot him a startled look. "Are you crazy?" she asked.

Colin shook his head seriously. "It's where I belong," he said.

When Alma started visiting Fort Devens, she could understand Colin's attraction to the army. She met other young couples who had made the army their careers. Liking their friendly community, she decided that maybe a military life wasn't so bad after all.

In August, Lieutenant Powell received new orders. "I'm going to Vietnam," he told Alma the next weekend.

"Oh, really?" she said.

"Yeah, and I'll be gone a year," Colin added.

"I don't want to tell you I'll be here when you get back," Alma told him. "I'm too old for that. I may write. I may not. But I don't really want to go through all of that."

The next weekend, Colin Powell went back to see Alma. "Okay," he said, "this is what we're going to do. We'll get married in two weeks. You'll go home next weekend to get ready for the wedding. I'll come down the week after that, and we'll get married."

That's exactly what they did. They called Alma's parents, who immediately started painting the house so it would be ready for the wedding. Friends started handwriting invitations for them. Alma went out and bought a wedding dress. And on August 24th they were married. Colin's old ROTC buddy and role-model, Ronnie Brooks, was the best man.

A month after the wedding, Colin Powell was sent to Fort Bragg, North Carolina, to take a six-week course before going to Vietnam. Since it was a temporary assignment, Alma was not authorized to go with her husband, and no quarters were available for them to live on base. Alma decided to go with Colin anyway. They spent several days looking for a place to live.

In the sixties, in many parts of the country, neighborhoods and apartment houses were segregated. Blacks could not live in the same neighborhoods as whites. Alma and Colin Powell had been offered only two places to live. One was a run-down house littered with old paint cans, sitting in the middle of a field people were using for a dump. The other was a small, dark, back room in somebody's house.

The Powells were very discouraged by the time they went to have dinner with Colin's friend Joe Schwar and his wife, Pat, later that evening. When they arrived, Joe was not yet back from work. Pat was preparing supper and tending three young children. When she heard their tale of woe, Pat promptly said, "Why don't you move in with us?"

Alma and Colin looked at each other, surprised. Pat had never met Alma before, she was busy with three young children, and yet she was offering them her home!

Just then Joe walked through the door. "Can't they, Joe?" Pat asked.

"What?" he replied.

"Can't the Powells move in with us?"

"Sure. When do they want to come?"

Alma excused herself to go to the bathroom. When she returned, Colin whispered to her, "Do they really have the room?" She delivered her scouting report—three bedrooms.

The Schwar boys, aged two and three, moved into the room with the four-month-old baby. The Powells moved into the boys' room, sleeping on their bunk beds for the next month and a half. They got along well together, living like one big happy family.

One day Alma and Pat went shopping together downtown. Pat stopped in front of a restaurant. "Let's go in and have a Coke," she suggested.

"You can go. I can't," Alma told her.

"What do you mean, you can't?" Pat asked.

"I can't go to that lunch counter," Alma explained. The restaurant, like the other eating places in the town, was segregated. Pat could eat there because she was white. Alma could not. Blacks were not allowed to eat there.

Another time, Alma, Colin, Pat, and Joe were sitting around after dinner. "Let's do something, you guys," Pat suggested. "Let's don't just sit here. Come on, let's go bowling."

Alma and Colin had to say no. "You can go," Alma told Pat. "We can't."

Even though segregation made her angry, there was little Pat could do about it. But she could show, by her own actions and example, what she thought was the right thing to do. She wouldn't listen to friends and neighbors who told her she shouldn't let the Powells live with her and her family. She could show them that people of different races could live together and help one another. The Schwars and the Powells are still close friends today, long after they shared that apartment at Fort Bragg.

The situation was even worse for Alma when she moved back to Birmingham, Alabama, to stay with her family while Colin Powell went to Vietnam. Birmingham in 1963 was a powder keg waiting to explode.

Almost half of Birmingham's citizens were black. But they did not have the same rights as the whites. White workers made more than twice as much money as black workers. Three times as many whites graduated from high school. Most whites were skilled workers. Most blacks worked at unskilled, manual labor.

Their families could not live in the same neighborhoods as whites. They couldn't eat in the same restaurants. Their children couldn't go to the same schools as the white children. They couldn't play in the same playgrounds. They had to ride in the back of public buses. They couldn't even use the same water fountains as whites.

In 1962, white city officials in Birmingham closed thirty-eight playgrounds, sixty-eight parks, six swimming pools, and four golf courses rather than allow blacks to use them with whites as a new federal law required. They thought it was better to do without these things themselves than to share them with blacks. The public library was opened to blacks, but all the chairs were removed so they couldn't sit there and read or study.

A black minister, the Reverend Fred Shuttlesworth, was whipped with a chain when he tried to enroll his daughter in a white school. His wife was stabbed in the same incident. Their house was leveled by a bomb.

Some people began to call Birmingham "Bombingham." If blacks moved too close to a white neighborhood, their houses might be bombed. One Sunday, four young black girls were killed when a bomb exploded in their church.

Dr. Martin Luther King and his followers organized a nonviolent march for equal rights in Birmingham. The white police fought back, loosing their dogs on them and battering them with nightsticks. Many of the protesters were jailed. Finally, so many adults were being arrested and losing the jobs they needed to support their families that King and his followers decided to get school children, aged six to eighteen, to join the protests. Unlike the adult protesters, the children would only miss school if they were arrested. The protest organizers also thought the police would not be as likely to hurt the children.

More than a thousand children stayed home from school to march. The children were met with ferocious police dogs and the fire department's high-pressure hoses. Children were thrown into the air, levelled to the ground, rolled down the street, tossed against parked cars, and slammed into trees by the force of the water. Americans across the

country were shocked when they saw the protest—
and what happened to the children—on TV.

Alma's father and uncle were the principals of
Birmingham's two black high schools. Every day
the demonstrators would come to the schools to
get the children, urging them to leave school and
go and march. Day after day, Alma's father had to
turn the demonstrators away at the door. "If their
mothers want them to march, let them come and
tell me," he told them. "But as long as the children
are in this building, I am responsible for them."

Even though they lived outside of central
Birmingham, Alma's family's home was not pro-
tected from the violence. One afternoon, not long
after her son Michael was born, Alma was hanging
diapers on the clothesline. She heard gunshots. A
black neighbor was returning home from work. As
he turned into his driveway, a car sped around the
corner and someone in the car took a couple of
shots at him.

Another time, Alma's father told her to put the
newborn Michael in an underground compartment
below the floor of the house. Then he handed her a
gun. "Anything that comes up that driveway, you
shoot first and ask questions later," he told her.

By the time Colin returned from Vietnam, the
situation at home had improved a little. President
Kennedy had sent in the National Guard to force
Alabama governor George Wallace to allow Bir-

mingham's schools to be integrated. Black children could attend the same schools as white children. The civil rights movement was strong, its progress slow but steady.

But there was still a long way to go. One day in 1964, Captain Colin Powell, an officer in the United States Army and a decorated veteran of Vietnam, went into Buck's Barbecue not far from Fort Benning, and ordered a hamburger.

"Are you an African student?" the waitress asked him.

"No," Captain Powell replied.

"Are you a Puerto Rican?" she asked.

"No," he said.

"You're Negro?"

"That's right," Powell answered.

"Well, I can't bring out a hamburger," the waitress told him. "We don't serve blacks out here. You'll have to go to the back door."

Captain Powell did not go to the back door. He left without the hamburger. Five months later, President Lyndon Johnson signed the Civil Rights Bill of 1964. Discrimination of all sorts was now illegal. Public restaurants could not be segregated. They could not serve some people and refuse to serve others. Captain Powell returned to Buck's Barbecue. He went in the front door. He sat at a table in the front. And he had his hamburger.

6

Jungle Patrol

The newlyweds Alma and Colin Powell spent Thanksgiving of 1962 together. But by Christmas they were on opposite sides of the world. Colin Powell, now a captain, left for Vietnam knowing that his wife was expecting a baby. Years later, he would understand how the men and women serving in the Gulf War felt about leaving their families behind. His first child would be born while he was thousands of miles away in the jungles of Vietnam.

Vietnam was divided into two sections. North Vietnam was the Socialist Republic of Vietnam. South Vietnam was noncommunist, called simply The Republic of Vietnam. The United States sent military advisors to South Vietnam to help the

South Vietnamese raise and train an army to protect themselves from the communists in the north. Captain Powell was one of those military advisors.

Taking little more than his field pack with him, Captain Powell traveled to a rugged, remote, mountainous area known as the A Shau Valley near Vietnam's border with Laos. The people who lived in the area were Montagnards or "mountain people." They were part of a civilian defense group trying to keep the North Vietnamese from coming into their country through Laos.

As an advisor to a Vietnamese army unit, Powell would go weeks at a time without seeing another American. A marine helicopter would bring food and mail to the remote area. Most of the time, Powell patrolled the jungle, looking for the enemy. These patrols would last days or weeks, and Captain Powell and the other men carried everything they needed with them.

On his head Powell wore a steel helmet with a canvas camouflage cover. Over his green fatigues he wore suspenders connected to a web belt. Attached to the belt were ammo pouches, grenades, and a couple of canteens. His pants legs were stuffed into his boots and sewn up tight to keep the jungle "critters" out. A poncho that doubled as a waterproof shelter when necessary was attached to his "ruck," the pack that carried the rest of his gear. A quick-release catch allowed the ruck to be dropped at a moment's notice in case of an ambush. Captain Powell was no longer riding around in a jeep or armored personnel carrier, watching the border as he had in the Fulda Gap in Germany. He was now a foot soldier, carrying a heavy M-14 rifle—what the army called "a lean, mean, green fighting machine."

Out on patrol, Powell slogged through swamps, over mountains, down valleys, and into jungles. Despite the heat, he wore his sleeves down because the razor-sharp elephant grass could cut flesh. Bloodsucking leeches fell from the trees and onto his head. The work was monotonous and never-ending. Walking. Starting and stopping. Looking for signs of the enemy. Keeping an eye out for snipers. Avoiding land mines that would maim or kill anyone who stepped on one.

Some patrols led to firefights with the Viet Cong. Most did not. But Captain Powell and his group were ambushed nearly every morning just before sun-up. Even when they couldn't find the enemy, the enemy always managed to find them.

Captain Powell was well-suited for the difficult and dangerous assignment of military advisor. He was physically fit and mentally tough. He was a proven leader, competent in tactics, and experienced with weapons. He was also diplomatic and culturally sensitive. He liked people and had grown

up accepting and respecting different cultures. He respected them, no matter what their background. He was willing to work with them, whoever they were.

On July 23, 1963, Captain Powell was out on patrol in the jungle as usual. He was trying to move forward to a vantage point so he could assist in deploying one of the batallion's rifle companies. Working his way through the dense undergrowth, he stepped into a pit where a simple but effective Viet Cong booby trap was hidden: a sharpened, poisoned bamboo stake called a "punji stick."

The point of a punji stick could puncture even the newest of army boots. The stick Powell stepped on went through the sole of his right boot. It went through the instep of his right foot. It passed all the way through the foot, missing all the bones, and came out through the top.

The wound didn't stop Captain Powell from completing his duties or making a two-hour hike back to the U.S. Special Forces camp. By the time he arrived, with the help of a makeshift cane, he was in severe pain, his foot an ugly purple and badly swollen. A medivac helicopter took him to the hospital at First Division Headquarters in Hue. But just a few weeks later, Captain Powell was back near the Laotian border, making jungle patrols and advising the South Vietnamese.

He received the Purple Heart medal for his

injury. And he was awarded a Bronze Star for his service and accomplishments during his first tour in Vietnam.

When Captain Powell was first assigned to Vietnam, there were 11,000 advisors. By the time he left a year later, the number of Americans in Vietnam had grown to 16,000. At the height of the war, five years later, more than 536,000 American men and women would be serving, and fighting, in Vietnam. Colin Powell was one of them.

When Captain Powell finished his first tour of Vietnam, he was assigned to Fort Benning, Georgia, again. Colin and Alma were reunited. Captain Powell was introduced to his six-month old son, Michael. This time the Powells were eligible for on-post officer's quarters. But there was a shortage of housing. Their names were put on a waiting list. Once more they found themselves looking for a place to live.

Even though Colin Powell was an army officer who had served in Vietnam, he still had trouble finding a home for his family. Being black limited his choices. For a while, Alma and the baby stayed in Birmingham with her family. Captain Powell would visit them on weekends and spend his off-duty time during the week looking for a house or apartment. Finally, he found a house to rent on 28th Avenue in Phoenix City, just over the Alabama border. It was their first real home together. In 1993, after Desert Storm and the Gulf War, 28th Avenue was renamed Colin Powell Avenue in his honor.

Captain Powell's new job at the U.S. Army Infantry Board wasn't exactly the height of excitement in his career, especially after a year in Vietnam. But the job was important. The Infantry Board's job was to test and retest all new equipment before it was given to the troops in the field. If a weapon or other piece of equipment didn't work the way it was supposed to, it could cost a soldier— or thousands of soldiers—their lives.

When a new rifle was developed, it was tested at the factory and then sent to the Infantry Board for testing at Fort Benning. There it would be fired, dragged through the mud, cleaned by troops, beat against the ground, and given a realistic field workout. Every new item a soldier might use was tested to be sure that it wouldn't fail the troops who would be using it later, in the field. Captain Powell was a test officer from November 1963 to June 1964 and again from May 1965 until February 1966. One of the main projects he worked on was testing and improving a new field radio.

Colin Powell had to take the Infantry Officer's Advanced Course, designed for those who intended to make the army their career. In the advanced course, captains were taught how to become company commanders. Captain Powell already had field experience working with the Vietnamese company commanders. He had already served on a company headquarters command-level staff in Vietnam.

Every class had long lists of information for the students to memorize. By the time Captain Powell got to the Advanced Course, he already knew much of what was being taught. Even so, he was a determined, hard-working student. His classmates remember him as a "team player." He wasn't a glory hound, always trying to make himself look better than the others. He always did his share of the work.

His superiors were impressed with him as well. After he completed the course and another assignment at the Infantry Board, Captain Powell was called back to Infantry school. This time he was an instructor himself.

Schoolhouse life was anything but the exciting life of a warrior. But, as always, Powell did the job he was given and did it the best that he could. Sometimes it was challenging. Classes were taught in large, dark lecture halls. Study groups met in smaller, windowless rooms. Most of Powell's classes were filled with tired, bored, impatient young men who knew they were on their way to fight the jungle war in Vietnam.

On Fridays, Powell had to teach one of the most tedious classes: how to fill out a unit-readiness report. Chairman Powell remembers it well. "You haven't lived," he says, "until you've tried to teach two hundred guys who have been up five straight days and nights, have just had a shower and a hot lunch, and are sitting in an air-conditioned room on a hot summer afternoon." He did anything he could to keep their attention—sometimes he even threw a rubber chicken at them. And he accomplished his assignment: The men in his class learned how to fill out a unit-readiness report.

In May 1966, while he was teaching and writing infantry training manuals, Captain Powell was promoted to the rank of major. He was selected "below the zone." That means that others who had first become officers at the same time he did were not yet being considered for promotion to major. Only a year after his promotion, Powell was also chosen to attend the army's Command and General Staff College (CGSC). This was an honor and an assignment usually reserved for more experienced majors and lieutenant colonels.

CGSC is offered only once a year at Fort Leavenworth, Kansas. At Leavenworth, Major Powell—the "average" student in grade school, high school, and City College—made his mark. When the course was over, he ranked second in a class of 1,244 officers.

By the time Powell finished CGSC, United States troops were no longer serving as advisors in Vietnam. They were actively engaged in fighting the war. By the end of 1967, nearly half a million Americans were "in country" in Vietnam. Sixteen thousand Americans had already been killed there. Among them was Colin Powell's close ROTC friend Tony Mavroudis, who had volunteered to go back to Vietnam.

7

Duty, Honor, Country

Major Powell returned to Southeast Asia himself in June 1968. He was assigned to be the 3/1 Infantry Batallion's executive officer. The 3/1 Infantry was deployed in Quang Ngai province. They were constantly playing hide-and-seek with the enemy. The Americans tried to root out and destroy command and communications posts. They searched for and tried to capture stores of enemy weapons and supplies. As they worked, the Viet Cong, who knew the jungles well and used them to their advantage, would harass the Americans with snipers, mines, and booby traps. Sometimes the two sides engaged in firefights, but most of the time it was a dangerous and deadly game of cat-and-mouse, hit-and-run.

The executive officer's job is to keep things going and support the fighting force in any way he can. He handles administrative activities. He oversees the commander's staff. His day is filled with making sure mail from home and necessities like "beans and bullets" get to the troops. He sees that vehicles are kept running and spare parts are ordered. He makes sure that log books are filled out and records are properly kept.

When Major Powell got to Quang Ngai, the batallion had been without an executive officer for two months. He created order and efficiency out of the chaos. Before he left, the unit was so highly rated in its annual general inspection it was selected to represent the entire Americal Division.

One day, the division commander, Major General Charles Gettys, was reading his copy of the weekly newspaper *Army Times* when he saw a story about the most recent Command and General Staff College graduating class. There in front of him was a picture of one of his officers, Major Colin Powell.

"I've got the number two Leavenworth graduate in my division and he's stuck out in the boonies?" Gettys exclaimed. "I want him on my staff!"

Major Powell was reassigned to division head-quarters. He found himself in the top war-fighting post on the general's staff. It was an important and difficult job, usually assigned to a higher-ranking officer. He had to work seven days a week, sometimes under hostile enemy fire, visiting the commanders and their troops. Most of the time he rode from place to place, visiting units with the division commander.

In November 1968, the 11th Infantry Brigade discovered twenty-nine North Vietnamese base camps. They captured one of the camps, deep in the woods outside the village of Quang Ngai, on November 15. It was an important victory because enemy maps and documents and a supply of weapons were captured.

Early the next afternoon, division commander Gettys decided to visit the newly captured base camp. His chief of staff, Colonel Jack Treadwell, his Operations Officer Colin Powell, two aides, and a four-man helicopter crew went with him. At 2:00 P.M. they arrived at a landing area that had just been freshly cut out of the jungle trees and undergrowth. They spotted the red smoke flare the ground crew had launched to mark the landing site.

But they didn't know that the brigade com-mander's helicopter had already tried, unsuccess-fully, to land in the same spot earlier that day. When his chopper was dropping down, almost vertically, the rotor blade had caught the tops of the trees surrounding the landing area. The pilot decided it was too tight to set down, so he flew to a more permanent, larger clearing nearby.

Gettys's pilot made several passes over the area, trying to decide on the best approach. Then he tried to take the chopper down. Thinking he was coming in too fast, the pilot circled off and tried again, much slower, from the north. The gunner told the pilot he was clear on his side. The crew chief told the pilot he was clear, but he needed to lift the tail up a little. The pilot started lowering the helicopter again.

Major Powell was sitting on the left side of the chopper, looking out the window at the tops of the thick jungle trees. Suddenly, the chopper jerked. Leaves and branches sprayed his window.

The chopper had hit the trees.

"I don't think we can make it!" the co-pilot shouted.

With a sickening crunch, the rotor blade caught on a tree trunk nearly six inches around. The chopper tilted left. Quickly, Powell and the other passengers bent over and grabbed their knees.

The helicopter plunged from the sky—twenty-five or thirty feet straight down. With a resounding crash that rocked the jungle, the chopper landed on its skids.

Major Powell and the gunner released their seatbelts. Powell burst out the side door as the engine started whining at a high pitch and began to smoke. PFC Bob Pyle, the gunner, was right on his heels.

"Get away! Get away! It's going to explode!" Major Powell shouted.

Glancing back, he saw that Colonel Treadwell and General Gettys were still trapped inside the helicopter. The pilots, whose doors could not be opened from the inside, were also still on board.

Pyle ran back to the helicopter. The pilot's door was crushed. Working in desperate haste, Pyle slid back the protective armor plate and jimmied the door open. But the pilot was still trapped—crushed in his seat by the armrest. Pyle worked feverishly to get him free.

Powell tried to run. He stumbled. Something was wrong with his ankle. Limping, his teeth clenched in pain, he ran back to the chopper and grabbed the general, who was barely conscious, and pulled him from the chopper. Others carried the general away.

The whining of the engine had intensified— like millions and millions of mosquitoes. Black smoke poured out of the broken machine. Choking from the oily fumes, Powell returned to the helicopter again. He reached for the colonel, who was bareheaded and bleeding from a wound to his head. He pulled the officer free and others carried him away as well.

For a third time, Major Powell went back to the chopper—this time for the general's aide. The aide was seated in the middle, right under the engine and transmission, which had smashed through the ceiling and had just missed crushing his head. His face battered by the radio, he moaned as Major Powell, the co-pilot, and the crew chief pried him out of the chopper.

Only two men remained, the pilot and the aviator. While Pyle pried the pilot from the crushed cabin, Powell pulled the aviator free of the wreckage.

Miraculously, everyone on board the helicopter survived. Just as amazing is the fact that Colin Powell had broken his ankle when the chopper first crashed. Ignoring his own painful injury, he had managed to get back to the chopper more than once and pull several of the others on board to safety. Today, General Powell is quick to point out that he wasn't alone and that many others were involved in the rescue of General Gettys and his crew. He says he didn't do anything heroic that day. But General Gettys thought otherwise. He saw to it that Major Colin Powell was awarded the Soldier's Medal, the army's award for bravery in non-combat situations.

Vietnam was not like Desert Storm. When the

United States troops went off to Saudi Arabia they were given huge farewells. The people at home, whether they knew the soldiers personally or not, tied yellow ribbons to fence posts, tree limbs, and mailbox poles, showing their support until the troops came home. They sent thousands of care packages, cards, and letters to the troops while they were away. Men and women returning from Desert Storm were treated like heroes.

More than 58,000 Americans died in Vietnam. Many Americans thought they never should have been there in the first place. While they fought in a jungle thousands of miles from home, people back in the United States marched in protest against the war. The returning Vietnam veterans had no parades, no welcomes. And they had no victory to celebrate. It took America twenty years to recognize its heroes—the young men and women who had gone when their country called, served bravely, sacrificed much, and given the best of themselves for duty, honor, and country.

Not long after the Desert Storm victory in Saudi Arabia, General Powell spoke to a group of fellow Vietnam veterans in front of the Vietnam Veterans' Memorial known as "The Wall." He told them about losing his close friend, Tony Mavroudis. Then he said, "You need no redemption. You redeemed yourself in the A Shau Valley. You redeemed yourself at Hue. You redeemed yourself at Dau Tieng, at Khe Sanh, in the South China Sea, in the air over Hanoi, or launching off Yankee Station, and in a thousand other places.

"The parades and celebrations are not needed to restore our honor as Vietnam veterans because we never lost our honor. They're not to clear up the matter of our valor because our valor was never in question. Two hundred and thirty-six Medals of Honor say our valor was never in question. Fifty-eight thousand, one hundred and seventy-five names on this wall say our valor and the value of our service were never in question."

Colin Powell

8

Taking Command

In September 1969, Colin Powell was back in the United States, in Washington, D.C. The army was sending him to school again. This time, he would not be studying "soldiering." He would be working on his master's degree in business administration at George Washington University.

In the late sixties, the anti-war movement was in full swing. In October, seventy-nine college presidents appealed to President Richard Nixon for a faster withdrawal of U.S. forces from Southeast Asia. In mid-November, a quarter of a million protesters marched from the Capitol up Pennsylvania Avenue to the Washington Monument. Across the country, young and old, rich and poor, black and white, students and workers from across the nation marched together in a variety of peaceful demonstrations opposing the war.

Major Powell did not get caught up in the protests and demonstrations or the debate over the Vietnam War. He was a soldier. He was in Washington to get a business degree. He hung out with other army and navy officers who were also in graduate school. He looked at graduate school as an opportunity to make good in a nonmilitary program. He never forgot that he had not been at the top of his class at CCNY. He was determined not to repeat his ho-hum performance.

The courses he liked the best were those that involved working with people—behavioral science and management. He got all A's except for one, a B in a computer programming course.

He was happy to be reunited with his wife, son, and young daughter. They bought a house in the Virginia suburbs. In the spring, his third child, Annemarie, was born. That summer, he was promoted to lieutenant colonel with a thirty-five-dollar-a-month increase in pay.

When he finished his degree program, Lieutenant Colonel Powell was assigned to the Pentagon— the headquarters for all the armed forces of the United States. The building itself is famous and unusual, with five sides, five floors, and five "rings" of office space on each floor. With six-and-a-half

Colin Powell

million square feet of floor space, its own indoor shopping mall and subway stop, sixty-seven acres of parking space, and offices for more than 24,000 people, the Pentagon is almost a city in itself

Two different offices wanted Lieutenant Colonel Powell on their staff: the assistant vice chief of staff's office, and the office of General William Dupuy, the army's number three officer at the Pentagon. Powell ended up working on General Dupuy's staff. He enjoyed the work and the people. But he was there only a short time before another assignment came along.

Early in 1972, Powell had been told that the army wanted him to apply for a White House Fellowship. Fellowships were open not just to the military, but to young professionals in a wide range of fields. Powell was given one weekend to fill out the eight pages of questions. Many of the questions required two-page answers. One of the questions involved writing a sample memorandum for the president that made a specific policy proposal. He sent the forms off and didn't give the application another thought.

A White House Fellowship is an honor and an opportunity. Over a thousand applications were received. Powell was among the one hundred thirty applicants who were invited for interviews. Then he was one of the thirty-three national finalists. At this point, Powell and his family were getting excited about the prospect of a fellowship. But the odds were still only fifty-fifty. Only half of the national finalists would end up with White House appointments.

The finalists spent three days at a conference center in Virginia being scrutinized in interviews and social situations. At the end of the weekend, the fellowship winners were announced. Powell was one of two African-Americans selected, one of only seventeen applicants chosen to become Fellows. One of the oldest and most experienced among them, Powell became one of the group's leaders as well.

Powell had interviews with several people, including the secretary of Health, Education, and Welfare and the director of the FBI. But finally he was appointed to the Office of Management and Budget, one of the most powerful offices in the United States government. There he met many powerful and important people, and he saw firsthand how politics and government worked. He also learned the importance of good public affairs—how to relate to the general public and how to handle the media. These things would come in handy later, when he became national security advisor and then chairman of the Joint Chiefs of Staff.

At the end of his fellowship year, the director of the Office of Management and Budget, Fred Malek, asked him to stay on. But Colin Powell had another "real army" job to do. It was time for a battalion command.

Ordinarily, Powell would have had to wait for a battalion. The number of commands is limited. Appointments are assigned by rank and seniority, and even the most highly qualified officers have to stand in line and wait their turn. But appointments to Korea were not as sought after as those in the United States or in Europe because they were "unaccompanied" one-year tours, meaning that officers could not take their wives and families. So when a command position with 2nd Infantry Division came up in Korea, Lieutenant Colonel Powell took it.

When Powell arrived, the division was in bad shape. The servicemen and women were abusing drugs, and racial tensions ran high. White troops had jumped a black soldier, and the blacks had retaliated. Some of the soldiers had served in Vietnam. They had come home to protests and demonstrations. Morale was at an all-time low.

In Korea, the Second Infantry Division was assigned to small, scattered posts that covered five hundred square miles. Powell's battalion was based on Camp Casey, also the site of the division headquarters. They were just south of the demilitarized zone—a neutral, non-combat area separating North and South Korea. Like the Fulda Gap that

Powell had guarded in Germany, it was the spot most likely to be involved in a confrontation. If North Korea decided to launch a war, Powell and his men would have been the first to meet the enemy. The atmosphere was tense, but the men had little to do but train and get into trouble in the towns nearby.

The division commander was Major General Hank "Gunfighter" Emerson. Major General Emerson thought that Powell might be able to bring the battalion—one of the worst in the division—under control. The battalion had been taken over by its own version of black street gangs. Emerson hoped that Powell, as a respected black officer, could earn the confidence and cooperation of the men serving under him.

Powell lost no time attacking the problem. Before long the gang leaders were punished under the Uniform Code of Military Justice. Others were court-martialled and tried in a military court of law. At the same time, Powell drew close to his junior officers, especially the young captains who were company commanders. He inspired their confidence and treated them with respect. He let the company commanders command their companies. And he set a good example of the sort of military and moral conduct he expected from his officers and men.

Swiftly and firmly, Powell tightened discipline.

Colin Powell

He ordered the men to think of themselves not as black men or white men but as soldiers, working together as a team. Meanwhile, Major General Emerson also cracked down on drug and racial problems. And he was ready to prove he meant what he said.

When the men were off duty, they went to two sections of the nearby town of Tongduchon. The whites would go to one section, and the blacks to another. The black section was called "the Crack." The black soldiers had warned the whites away. "Don't nobody come in here, or else," they said.

One night Emerson called together Lieutenant Colonel Powell and his other batallion commanders. "We're all going to the Crack tonight," he told them. "And if anything happens, we're going to take the whole division in there and clean it out."

The commanders all went down to the Crack. "Enjoy yourselves," Emerson told them. "You don't have to mix with whites or blacks—it's a personal choice. But we're soldiers." He expected the officers and troops under his command to act like soldiers and treat each other the same way.

The major general tightened up the training, making the men run four miles every morning. Then he kept them busy, hard at work, all day long. By the time night came, the troops were too exhausted to think about drugs or get into trouble.

Through hard work and strict discipline, Lieutenant Colonel Powell's battalion developed into a tough, disciplined fighting unit. He had taken a rag-tag bunch of men in fatigues and turned them into a fighting force ready for whatever they might face in combat. He had also proved himself to be a first-rate field officer. Major General Emerson rated Colin Powell as one of the top two of his sixty-five batallion commanders.

9

General Powell

One evening while Maud Powell was visiting her son and his family, Colin Powell asked everyone to gather around the table for a family meeting. His children looked at him, surprised. They'd never had a family meeting before. But obediently they seated themselves at the dining room table and waited to hear what he had to say.

Colin Powell looked at them each in turn—his mother, his wife, and his children. "I just want to tell you this," he said. "Today the president said that I get to be a general."

It took a moment for the news of his promotion to sink in. Then Maud Powell jumped up and excitedly embraced Colin. Her son had spent twenty-one years in uniform, and he was being promoted to one-star general! All her doubts about his career had proved unfounded. A short time later, when Colin's first star was pinned on, Maud looked on proudly.

General Colin Powell and his family had returned to Washington, D.C. With long separations and frequent moves from place to place, army life can be hard on a family. The Powells were happy to be settled together again.

Their oldest child, Michael, was a teenager at the time. "I always admired my father," Mike remembers, "but he worked a lot. He was on the job night and day. And then there was the Korea tour and Vietnam when he went away." The move to Washington gave him a chance to get closer to his father.

Mike remembers when he turned sixteen. "I got this long letter from my father. It must have been twelve or fifteen pages." The letter was sent anonymously, and Colin Powell never asked Mike if he had read it. But Mike knew it was from his father. He had written, "Just remember that the next four years are the most important four years you are ever going to experience. Remember that your mother and I have shown you right from wrong, and now the rest is up to you. You don't do things according to our wishes. *You* make the decision of whether it's right or wrong in accord with the ways that we taught you." The letter concluded with the words, "Never forget, there is nothing too bad that you can't come and get our help."

Aside from right and wrong, the Powells tried to teach their children a sense of responsibility. Although they knew they could always count on their parents' support, Mike and his sisters also knew they couldn't come and tell their parents, "I messed things up. Fix it for me." The first thing their parents would want to know is what they tried to do about the problem themselves.

"You would get in more trouble for not taking responsibility for your mistakes than for the mistakes themselves," Mike says. One time, as a teenager, he ran out of gas. He left the car in the middle of the street and walked home. His father scolded him—but not for running out of gas. He scolded Mike for not being responsible enough to move the car out of traffic.

At the time, General Colin Powell was taking on more and more responsibilities himself. As he had when he was a teenager, and later as a young soldier, Colin Powell began moving up from one job to the next, earning more important and more challenging new positions because of how well he had done the job before. And it seemed like every time he got a new "real army" position, someone was calling him back to Washington again.

First, John Kester, special assistant to Jimmy

Carter's secretary of defense, was looking for a military assistant. He wanted someone he could depend on to get things done. When he read about Powell's background, he liked what he saw: a White House Fellowship. A proven soldier and commander. Vietnam War decorations. Experience at the Pentagon.

Powell was with his brigade out in the woods on a field training exercise when he got a call on the field phone inviting him to come to Washington for an interview.

Powell handled himself well. He was confident and comfortable. Most of all, his straightforward answers impressed Kester.

At one point in the interview, Powell asked Kester, "How did you happen to bring me in here?"

Kester replied, "I checked you out. And I heard a lot of good things about you."

"Well, as a matter of fact, I checked you out too," Powell told him. He grinned at Kester. "And it wasn't all good."

Six men interviewed for the job. Kester chose Powell.

Later, President Carter's deputy director of defense, Charles Duncan, asked General Powell to become his chief military assistant. Duncan says he liked three things in particular about Colin Powell: He worked extremely well with people. He was a fast learner. And he had enormous energy and stamina.

When Ronald Reagan became president after Jimmy Carter, he named Caspar Weinberger as his secretary of defense and Frank Carlucci as his deputy secretary. Colin Powell stayed on as their chief military assistant for five months. Then he had a chance to return to the army and be the number-two soldier in a division. He jumped at the opportunity to take on a command position again.

General Powell went to Fort Carson, Colorado, to serve as the 4th Mechanized Infantry Division's assistant division commander for operations and training. Then he went back to Fort Leavenworth to serve as deputy commanding general there. He stayed at Fort Leavenworth for eleven months. And he earned a second star. Then Caspar Weinberger called him back to Washington again.

It was a tense and exciting time to be working at the U.S. Defense Department. There seemed to be one crisis after another: Iran and Iraq were at war in the Middle East, in the same area where the United States would later fight in Desert Storm.

The Soviets downed a Korean jetliner, claiming it was on a spy mission. Then they blamed the tragedy that took 269 lives on the United States. More than two hundred Marines were killed when a suicide terrorist drove a truck carrying a ton of explosives into the U.S. Marine headquarters in Beirut, Lebanon.

The United States Marines landed on the tiny

Caribbean island of Grenada to help restore democracy. TWA flight 847 was hijacked by a radical group of Moslems and a passenger, navy diver Robert Stethem, was murdered. The United States made air strikes on targets in Libya after Libyan terrorists bombed a bar in Germany and killed several American soldiers.

In 1986, General Powell left the Office of the Secretary of Defense for Germany. He had begun his career in the same place. His first time in Germany, he had commanded forty men, sitting in the Fulda Gap, keeping an eye on the Soviet Guards Army. Now he commanded the 72,000 soldiers of V Corps.

No sooner had Powell settled in Germany than he got a call from Frank Carlucci. He had worked for Carlucci at the Department of Defense. Now, Ronald Reagan had asked Carlucci to be his new National Security Advisor. And Carlucci wanted Colin Powell to be his Deputy Advisor.

General Powell didn't want to leave his new command so soon. "I don't want to come back to Washington," he told Carlucci.

The next night, Powell's home phone rang shrilly, a sure sign of a call from the White House operators. He answered the phone.

It was President Reagan. "I know you've been looking forward to this command," he said, "but we need you here."

"Mr. President," Powell answered, "I'm a soldier, and if I can help, I'll come."

So once again General Powell packed up and returned to Washington. As deputy advisor, he would advise Frank Carlucci and the president on when to use military force and the cost and consequences involved in any such decision.

When Caspar Weinberger resigned as secretary of defense, the president asked Frank Carlucci to take the cabinet post. The choice of a new national security advisor to replace Carlucci was not a difficult one. Everyone seemed to agree there was only one man for the job. In 1987, General Colin Powell became the first and only black to become assistant to the president for national security affairs.

President Reagan trusted Colin Powell's opinion and advice. "Finding someone who will talk straight to you in Washington is a rare and valuable asset," the president said of Powell. On a photo he signed for the general he wrote, "Dear Colin, If you say it's so, then I know it's OK."

Along with his other duties as national security advisor, Colin Powell helped to coordinate a number of important summit meetings between President Reagan and other world leaders. But he thought our national security depended on more than diplomacy and military might. Three issues that concern most Americans today concerned him then: improving the economy, protecting the environment, and providing a sound education for our children. Powell thought if we worked on those three things, our nation—and our world—would be more secure.

When George Bush became president, he offered Colin Powell his choice of positions in the new government. He could take over as director of the CIA (Central Intelligence Agency). Or he could be the deputy secretary of state. Powell chose to return to the army, accepting a four-star promotion and the largest command in the United States military. But his stay as head of the Forces Command near Atlanta, Georgia, was a short one.

As vice president, George Bush had admired Powell's work, especially how he ran meetings. "He'd run them and get them over with in a hurry," Bush said. "He was thorough, and he presented people's positions very, very fairly and objectively. He was crisp and strong, even with the president."

So when the position of the chairman of the Joint Chiefs of Staff opened, President Bush asked General Powell to come back to Washington to serve as his chief military advisor. Some of Bush's advisers argued against Powell's appointment as chairman. They thought that he didn't have quite enough experience to win the confidence of his colleagues. But George Bush said, "I decided that because of Colin's *character* and the way he works

with people, he would have the confidence of the others from day one. And I think history will show that he certainly did."

A chairman of the Joint Chiefs of Staff does not command troops, but he is the highest ranking officer in all the armed forces. His responsibilities are great. He serves as the chief military advisor to the president, the national security council, and the secretary of defense. He is also the head of the Joint Chiefs of Staff, made up of the top officers in the army, navy, air force, and marines. With the Joint Staff, a group of 1,600 military and civilians, the chairman develops the military's strategic plans.

When General Colin Powell was sworn into office on October 1, 1989, he became the youngest man, and the first black, to become chairman of the Joint Chiefs of Staff.

10

A Test of Faith

Going to church and participating in church activities has always been a part of Chairman Powell's life. His mother and father had been very involved in church activities. Their faith and the religious education of their children were important to them.

Colin Powell still remembers his confirmation. He tells of the bishop laying his hands on his head and saying this traditional prayer: "Defend, O Lord, this Thy child with Thy heavenly grace; that he may continue Thine forever; and daily increase in Thy Holy Spirit more and more, until he comes unto Thy everlasting kingdom. Amen."

"These words gave me a deep assurance,"

said Powell. "After that, every time I heard those words, I knew that God was watching over me. And I knew that I needed to live up to his expectations."

As a boy in South Bronx, Colin was an acolyte at St. Margaret's Episcopal Church. When Major Powell and his wife bought a home in Virginia, the whole family became active members of another St. Margaret's, in Woodbridge. Alma was involved in the Altar Guild. Mike became an acolyte like his father had been. Colin Powell eventually became the senior warden of the church.

Later, as a brigade commander concerned about the spiritual welfare of his soldiers, Powell would attend the Episcopal service with his family each Sunday. Then he would return to the unit chapel and attend the different worship services his troops might be attending. These services ranged from black Baptist to Pentecostal, from Catholic Mass to a nondenominational Protestant service. He was showing both his own faith and his support for their decision to worship in whatever way they thought best.

Even as chairman of the Joint Chiefs of Staff, Colin Powell was not afraid to be publicly identified as a man of God. After reviewing the Old Guard troops in the ceremony marking his appointment as chairman, Powell described an enormous painting that he passes each day as he walks the halls of the Pentagon.

It is a picture of the inside of the Strategic Air Command chapel, painted in the early 1960s by Woodi Ishmael. In the painting, bright sunlight is streaming through a stained glass window, coloring the faces of a small family—father, mother, son, and daughter—kneeling at the altar rail. The father is in uniform. Together, they are praying for his safe return from war and for the strength to face whatever might lie ahead.

"Every time I pass that painting a silent prayer comes to mind for all of those who serve this nation in times of danger," the new chairman said. Throughout the Gulf War, General Powell prayed fervently for "his kids," the young servicemen and women who served under him.

Chairman Powell publicly praised the work of the International Bible Society, which had provided low-cost Bibles for the troops who served in Operation Desert Shield. "The Bibles you distributed to our men and women in uniform," General Powell said, "were a testament to the spiritual need that must be met on the battlefield."

However, one of General Powell's biggest tests of faith came not in the Gulf War, but in a family tragedy.

His only son, Mike Powell, had followed in his father's footsteps. Although he had been accepted at West Point, he decided to go to Thomas Jefferson's alma mater—the College of William and Mary. He enrolled in ROTC and was graduated and commissioned a second lieutenant in May, 1985. His father presided at the commissioning ceremony. After he was given his commission, Mike Powell saluted his father. His father returned the salute.

Two years later, First Lieutenant Mike Powell was serving in Germany as an executive officer for a cavalry troop. Returning from a day-long reconnaissance mission, Mike and two other men were in the fourth and last army vehicle in their convoy.

In the early evening, tired out from his long day of duty, the driver of Mike's M151 jeep began to doze. His head nodded, then snapped up. Eyes now open, he saw that he was drifting toward the guardrail. Quickly he jerked the wheel sharply to the left. The wheels of the jeep squealed—and the jeep headed directly into the oncoming lane of traffic.

Seeing a truck coming toward them, the driver pulled at the wheel again, jerking it in the opposite direction. Still going sixty miles an hour, the army jeep swerved out of control, just missing a head-on collision before it flipped side-over-side. The driver's side went down and Mike Powell's side of the vehicle came over it.

Mike was thrown into the air and landed on the road. The jeep landed on top of him and continued spinning, right side over left, leaving Mike's broken body lying in the road.

Within minutes a German ambulance arrived. The other lieutenant had, miraculously, suffered only minor injuries. He was up and walking around. The driver was hurt. And Mike Powell was in very serious condition.

When the medical team got him to the hospital, the doctors wanted to give him up for dead. The weight of the jeep had crushed and snapped his pelvis, broken his lower back, and given him massive internal injuries. The other lieutenant who had been in the jeep with him convinced the doctors to do everything they could for Mike until a helicopter could take him to a U.S. Army Hospital.

Back home in the United States, Colin and Alma Powell got a long-distance call. "Your son has been in an accident—a very serious one," they were told. "He is near death."

The Powells wanted to get to Germany as quickly as possible to be near their son. So they gratefully accepted President Reagan's offer of an air force aircraft to fly them there. When they arrived, they found Mike rigged with several intravenous bottles, dripping blood, medicine, and water into his veins. The troops from his unit had made a special trip to the hospital to donate the large amounts of blood he needed for his transfusions. His body was so swollen with fluids that the Powells couldn't even recognize their son.

Mike's parents met with his doctor. "His condition is critical," the doctor told them, his face solemn. "We do not expect him to live."

"We expect him to live," Alma and Colin replied. "And we expect you to do everything you can for our son."

Colin and Alma Powell did not give up easily. Praying fervently for Mike's recovery, they supervised his transfer to Walter Reed Army Hospital in Washington, D.C. Alma stayed with her son around the clock, and Colin spent as much time with Mike as he could manage away from the White House each day.

Surgery fused the discs in Mike's lower spine. In July, doctors used a special steel frame to hold his pelvis together. The road to recovery was long and difficult. Mike constantly battled life-threatening infections, and he underwent numerous surgeries. For long months, his condition remained critical.

But Colin and Alma Powell's prayers were answered. Mike did not die. He had to stay in the hospital for nine months. The steel frame held his pelvis together until it was safe to remove it in October. Since his accident, he has had surgery fourteen times. When he left the hospital, he got a medical retirement from the army.

Out of the tragedy came a special joy for the Powell family. In college, Mike had dated a classmate, Jane Knott. When they graduated and Second Lieutenant Powell went off to the army, she and Mike were still good friends. When she heard about the accident, Jane came to be with Mike every day. As the months in the hospital went on and on, other friends came less and less often to see him, but Jane continued to visit Mike every day. Mike and Jane were married seven months after his release from the hospital, in October 1988.

Mike's first ambition in life was to have an army career like his father. When he was only six years old, he wrote a letter to his father in Vietnam. It said, "Dear Dad, I hope everything is fine. I'm fine. Mom's fine. We miss you. Right now I don't know what I want to be when I grow up, either a lieutenant colonel in the army or a lawyer. Come home soon. We miss you. Michael."

Few people believed Mike would survive the terrible injuries he suffered in the jeep accident. But neither he nor his family ever gave up. Mike survived. He learned to walk again. He got married and started a family of his own. But because of his accident, Mike had to give up his dream of an army career. He decided to pursue his second goal instead. In May 1993, he finished law school at Georgetown University.

Colin Powell

11

Desert Storm

Although he has been a soldier most of his life, Colin Powell says, "War is the tool of last resort." Sometimes, though, when all else fails, countries, like people, have to be willing to stand up and fight for what they believe in.

On August 2, 1990, hundreds of Iraqi tanks invaded the smaller neighboring country of Kuwait. The people of Kuwait were no match for Iraq's huge army or its sophisticated modern weapons. Iraqi troops seized control of the Kuwait government. The leader of Iraq, Saddam Hussein, declared Kuwait to be part of his country.

Saddam Hussein gave the people of Kuwait a choice. They could surrender and accept defeat.

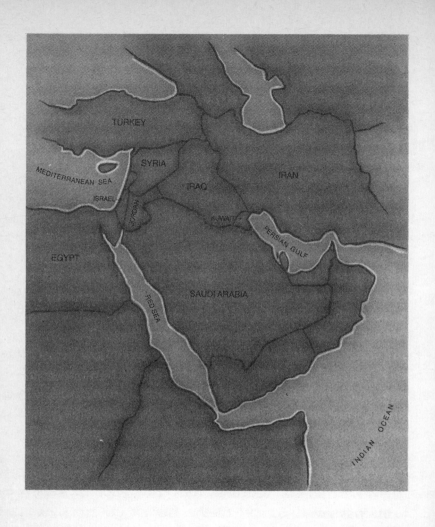

They could obey his laws and accept his dictatorship. Or he would turn their country "into a graveyard." He didn't think the people of Kuwait could do anything about it. He didn't think the rest of the world would try. He didn't think the United States would be willing to risk thousands of American lives for a tiny country so far from home. He was wrong.

The countries of the United Nations protested. They demanded Iraq's withdrawal from Kuwait. Saddam Hussein ignored their demands.

Countries around the world broke off relations with Iraq. They quit buying Iraq's oil. The United Nations again condemned Saddam Hussein's actions in Kuwait. They declared a ban on all trade with the country. Nothing, except food and medical supplies, could go in or out of the country. Even the Soviet Union, an ally of Iraq in the past, voted in favor of the bans. Saddam Hussein still ignored them. He refused to leave Kuwait.

Saudi Arabia, another neighbor of Iraq, agreed to close the oil pipeline Iraq needed to get its oil supply to market. In return, they asked the United States to protect them against the larger, stronger, better equipped Iraqi army. They realized that Iraq might attack them next to gain control of their huge, prosperous oil wells.

Thousands of U.S. troops began moving into Saudi Arabia. They were there to form a "Desert

Shield" between that country and Iraq. Forty other countries began sending troops and equipment as well. Even though Saddam Hussein tried to make it look like a "holy war"—Moslems against Christians and Jews—even Arab countries like Egypt and Syria joined the international alliance against him. Saddam Hussein still refused to budge. He would not take his army out of Kuwait.

The standoff lasted almost five months. The United Nations had given Hussein a deadline and an ultimatum. "A line has been drawn in the sand," President Bush said. "Withdraw from Kuwait unconditionally and immediately, or face the terrible consequences." Saddam Hussein ignored the warnings again. The United Nations deadline came and went unheeded.

On January 15, the United States and its allies began air strikes against Iraq's forces. They bombed Iraqi ships and aircraft, missile launchers, and weapons supplies. The allies wanted to make sure that Saddam Hussein would not be able to use his chemical weapons or build a nuclear bomb. They had to prevent Saddam Hussein from taking over other countries in the Middle East and from seizing control of the world's oil supplies. Bombs flashed above the city of Baghdad, and "Desert Shield" became "Desert Storm."

The allied plan was simple. In a press conference, Chairman Powell explained exactly what the allies intended to do with the Iraqi army. "First we're gonna cut it off, then we're gonna kill it," he said.

The allies flew 3000 missions a day and dropped 90,000 tons of explosives on the enemy. Then, on February 24, ten armored divisions rolled into the Iraqi desert to begin the ground war against Iraq. On February 25, Saddam Hussein ordered his army to retreat from Kuwait City. They fled with the loot they had taken from Kuwait stores, homes, and people, and tried to take their weapons and equipment with them.

But the allied army cut off their retreat and kept the forces and their munitions from getting back into Iraq. On February 27, Kuwaiti troops raised the Kuwaiti flag in Kuwait City. President Bush addressed the nation. "Kuwait is liberated," he told the American people and the world. "Iraq's army is defeated." The war was over.

Many people think Desert Storm was one of the greatest military victories in American history. The Gulf War ended less than six weeks after it began. Allied casualties totalled less than a hundred. Just as importantly, it was a unified effort. Many nations of the world, both large and small, joined together to rescue Kuwait and stop Saddam Hussein.

The war also proved that America's peacetime forces were combat ready and able. It put our sophisticated weapons, like the cruise missiles and

Stealth fighter-bombers, to their first real test, proving that they worked and we knew how to use them.

What was Colin Powell's role during Desert Shield and Desert Storm? As chairman of the Joint Chiefs of Staff, his main job, as always, was to advise the president of the United States.

One of the most serious decisions a president can make is whether or not he should send troops into combat. This one decision can affect—and cost—hundreds of thousands of lives. When George Bush had to decide whether or not to send troops to Saudi Arabia, or whether to start the air strikes, or when to order the land offensive, it was Colin Powell's duty as chairman to see that the president had all the information he needed to make the best decision. He would lay out all the alternatives, and they would discuss the possible consequences. Finally, President Bush would make the final decision.

Once the war began, Chairman Powell made sure that all the armed services were represented fairly and completely and that the concerns and opinions of all branches of the military were heard and answered. This is what he means when he says the chairman is "purple suited." The chairman isn't supposed to represent only one color of uniform— air force blue, navy blue, or his own army green. He's there to represent them all.

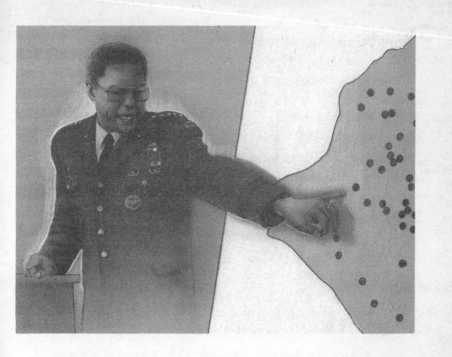

Finally, Chairman Powell had one other role. After the war, a young cadet at the United States Naval Academy asked Chairman Powell how he felt about his role as "a go-between between the politicians and General Schwarzkopf."

Chairman Powell laughed his distinctive, hearty laugh. "Without fear of being a little immodest, I was slightly more than a go-between," he responded. "But your characterization is not bad."

As a go-between, Powell was a strong link in the chain of command. He linked General Schwarzkopf and the secretary of defense with the president, who is the commander in chief of all the United States armed forces. And he linked the government officers and officials and the American people. "Trust me," he told the reporters and the American public during a press briefing. And they did.

Most Americans think of people like Colin Powell and General Schwarzkopf when they think of the heroes of Desert Storm. But General Powell would disagree. He says that in the military—as in any family, or in life in general—all jobs are important. Success in war belongs to those who serve in a cockpit or a tank or a foxhole or on a ship. To Chairman Powell, the real heroes of Desert Storm were "his kids"—those who put their lives on the line for their country.

One of the Desert Storm heroes Chairman

Powell talks about is Private First Class Frank Bradish. Bradish was a soft-spoken, quiet young teenager from Idaho when he went to Saudi Arabia. In the middle of the night, his Bradley Fighting Vehicle was hit by enemy fire. Bradish was wounded in both legs. He lost several of his fingers. But his injuries didn't keep him from going in and pulling his buddies out of the burning personnel carrier.

Bradish wanted to signal to the medics so they would come to tend his wounded friends. With mangled hands, he worked feverishly to twist the cap off of the signal flare. Finally, he bent down and bit off the cap with his teeth. Then he crawled back into the burning vehicle to get out the ammunition that had been left inside. He was afraid it would explode and kill everyone. Only when some other soldiers pulled him out of the vehicle did Bradish look down and see that he was seriously injured and bleeding badly.

Another story Powell tells is when ABC reporter Sam Donaldson interviewed some of the Desert Storm troops in Saudi Arabia. First Donaldson talked to Corps Commander Lieutenant General Freddy Franks, who had had a leg blown off in Vietnam. Then Donaldson interviewed some of the soldiers who served together in the First Armored Division. White soldiers. African-American soldiers. Hispanic-American soldiers. Asian-American soldiers. Young soldiers and veteran soldiers. Men and women.

One young African-American soldier, about nineteen, said to Donaldson, "All these guys right here are my family." And his buddies all grunted and shouted in agreement behind him.

That sense of family is what won the Gulf War, says Colin Powell. The bedrock of warfare, he says, is "trusting people, working as a team, being a family." In a military manual on how to fight and win a war, he wrote: "When a team takes to the field, all players try to do their very best because every other player, the team, and the home town are counting on them to win. So it is when the armed forces of the United States go to war. We must win every time. Every soldier must take the battlefield believing his or her unit is the best in the world. Every pilot must take off believing there is no one better in the sky. Every sailor standing watch must believe there is no better ship at sea. Every marine must hit the beach believing that there are no better infantrymen in the world. But they must also believe that they are part of a team, a joint team, that fights together to win. This is our history, this is our tradition, this is our future."

Colin Powell is proud of "his kids" who served in Desert Storm. "They'll die for each other. They'll die for their duty," he says. He's quick to point out their strengths. He says they're smart, dedicated, well-trained, and motivated. They're also responsible, reliable, self-confident, and selfless. They're patriotic, tolerant, and caring. And they are the true heroes of Desert Storm.

Colin Powell has seen what service in the military can do for a young man or woman. He knows how it changed his own life. He thinks that more of our youth—especially those who are poor and live in dangerous inner-city areas—can use that sort of pride, spirit, and self-confidence.

That's why he supports military teaching in the schools. Programs are already in place in more than 1500 secondary schools across America where military subjects are taught by retired and reserve officers. General Powell would like to see that number grow to 9000.

"It's a wonderful way to get role models back into our schools," the general says, "to show youngsters what it means to be a good American, what it means to work hard and achieve success." That's exactly the sort of role model General Colin Powell has been himself.

12

"It Can Be Done"

Even a hero has heroes. Colin Powell's heroes have always tended to be "ordinary" people who turned out to be extraordinary—his parents, the family and friends he knew growing up, the troops with whom he has served.

Among the more famous people he admires are Thomas Jefferson, who wrote the Declaration of Independence and helped define what American democracy is all about; Abraham Lincoln, who wrote the Emancipation Proclamation; and Martin Luther King, who was not afraid to stand up for what he believed, no matter what personal price he had to pay. These were men who saw something wrong with society and tried to fix it. That's the sort of person, famous or not, that Colin Powell admires.

General Powell likes to fix things, too, whether it's the old Volvo cars he fixes on weekends, or a battalion of troops who are not all they can be, or a complicated international situation in which the president and the nation are counting on his information and advice.

Some people think he should run for president. All General Powell will say about his retirement from the army is that he is going to spend more time with his family, keep on fixing Volvos, and "go out and run something."

At first glance, Colin Powell might seem to be a man of contradictions. He's devoted his life to a career in the military, but his favorite Bible passage is 1 Corinthians 13, the passage on love. He's a very private man who likes to keep "a low profile," but he's often in the public eye. He wears old suits and drives old station wagons and prefers simple things like listening to music on the radio and eating hamburgers, but he's spent much of his life with the world's richest and most powerful people. He keeps his private politics and opinions to himself, not letting them influence his work or his professional decisions, but some of the most important leaders in our country have depended heavily on his advice.

Colin Powell has served several United States presidents—Carter, Reagan, Bush, and Clinton— and served them well, but he's not afraid to disagree with the commander in chief when he feels a decision is not a good one. When Clinton became president, Chairman Powell opposed some of the changes the new president wanted to make in the military.

Once, General Powell was interviewed for an article in *Inside Journal,* a newspaper that is read by more than a quarter million men and women in prison. When the article came out in the paper, it was titled, "He's Cool, He's Tough, and He Works Like a Dog," which is a pretty good description of the general.

In the article, the interviewer said, "Many young people are prisoners today because of the lure of easy money through drugs as opposed to hard work. A big part of your message is the value of work."

Colin Powell replied, "Everywhere I've gone, I've tried to make that point. I don't know successful people who don't work hard. Success is hard work."

He continued, "Many interviewers come and sit with me and say, 'Gee, how did you do it?' Worked like a dog! That's how I did it. I work very, very hard. I always have. I worked hard when I was mopping floors. I've worked ever since I was fifteen years old. I was never without a job. Most of the time it was pure manual labor while I was in college and high school. When I got out of college I joined the army, and I've worked very hard for thirty-four years since then."

Colin Powell went on to encourage anyone who wants to make something better of himself. No matter what your situation, you can make something of your life, he said. Refuse to accept the view others have of you. Attach yourself to something positive—family, church, or school. Be your own person and make your own decisions. Don't give up.

Colin Powell has put this advice into action in his own life. The son of hard-working immigrant parents, he grew up at a time when minority youths were not given the same opportunities or encouraged to follow the same dreams as white children. He became the highest ranking soldier in America, a man trusted and respected by people of all ages, races, and backgrounds.

When he was a child, people thought he was "slow" and "average." He refused to accept their opinion. Surrounded by pressures to join neighborhood street gangs and get into drugs, he attached himself instead to positive things—family, church, a career in the army. He was his own person, making his own decisions. He found a goal and stuck to it. He didn't give up.

Colin Powell says he believes in several things. He believes in the country we live in. He believes in democracy, in government of the people, by the people, for the people. He believes in his family. He believes in himself. And he believes that God gave us a life to use for a purpose.

There's one other thing that Colin Powell believes in. It's his motto—the words he lives by. It's something he has proven in his own life and career—something he'd like young people to remember when they find a goal they'd like to achieve or a dream they'd like to follow. His motto?

If you work at something hard enough, it can be done.